THE BOOK OF ANSWERS

CAROL BOLT

NEW YORK

Hyperion and the author of this book
take no credit or responsibility for what
The Book of Answers
advises or the results thereof.

All rights reserved. No part of this book may be used
or reproduced in any manner whatsoever without
the written permission of the Publisher.
Printed in the United States of America. For information address:
Hyperion, c/o ABC, 77 West 66th Street, New York, New York 10023-6298

Designed by KimShala Wilson

Library of Congress Cataloging-in-Publication Data
ISBN 0-7868-6566-0
FIRST EDITION
10 9 8 7 6 5 4

How to Use
The Book of Answers

1. Hold the **closed** book in your hand, on your lap, or on a table.

2. Take 10 or 15 seconds to **concentrate** on your question. Questions should be phrased **closed-end**, e.g. " Is the job I'm applying for the right one?" or "Should I travel this weekend?"

3. While visualising or speaking your question (one question at a time), place **one hand** palm down on the book's front cover and **stroke the edge** of the pages, back to front.

4. When you **sense** the time is right, **open** the book and there will be your answer.

5. **Repeat** the process for as many questions as you have.

Got questions? This book has the answers.

Carol Bolt is a professional artist living in Seattle.
This is her first book.

YOUR ACTIONS WILL
IMPROVE THINGS

DON'T BET ON IT

ADOPT
AN ADVENTUROUS ATTITUDE

FOLLOW THE ADVICE OF EXPERTS

YOU COULD FIND YOURSELF
UNABLE TO COMPROMISE

FOCUS ON YOUR HOME LIFE

INVESTIGATE AND THEN ENJOY IT

DEFINITELY

IT WILL REMAIN UNPREDICTABLE

ABSOLUTELY NOT

EXPLORE IT
WITH PLAYFUL CURIOSITY

BE DELIGHTFULLY SURE OF IT

BETTER TO WAIT

IT SEEMS ASSURED

DO IT EARLY

KEEP IT TO YOURSELF

STARTLING EVENTS
MAY OCCUR AS A RESULT

THE ANSWER MAY COME TO YOU
IN ANOTHER LANGUAGE

YOU WILL NEED
TO ACCOMMODATE

DOUBT IT

IT WILL BRING GOOD LUCK

BE PATIENT

YOU WILL FIND OUT EVERYTHING
YOU'LL NEED TO KNOW

THERE IS A SUBSTANTIAL LINK TO ANOTHER SITUATION

WATCH AND SEE WHAT HAPPENS

IT WILL AFFECT
HOW OTHERS SEE YOU

YOU'LL BE HAPPY YOU DID

GET IT IN WRITING

UNFAVORABLE AT THIS TIME

UPGRADE ANY WAY YOU CAN

IF YOU DO AS YOU'RE TOLD

IF IT'S DONE WELL;
IF NOT, DON'T DO IT AT ALL

DON'T ASK FOR ANY MORE
AT THIS TIME

AVOID THE FIRST SOLUTION

YOU'LL GET THE FINAL WORD

PROCEED AT A MORE
RELAXED PACE

THE BEST SOLUTION
MAY NOT BE THE OBVIOUS ONE

REMAIN FLEXIBLE

THAT'S OUT OF YOUR CONTROL

PROVIDED YOU SAY
"THANK YOU"

ENJOY THE EXPERIENCE

APPROACH CAUTIOUSLY

PAY ATTENTION TO THE DETAILS

WATCH YOUR STEP AS YOU GO

SPEAK UP ABOUT IT

DON'T HESITATE

THIS IS A GOOD TIME TO
MAKE A NEW PLAN

MOVE ON

THERE IS NO GUARANTEE

THE CIRCUMSTANCES
WILL CHANGE VERY QUICKLY

DON'T GET CAUGHT UP
IN YOUR EMOTIONS

SHIFT YOUR FOCUS

IT IS SIGNIFICANT

REPRIORITIZE
WHAT IS IMPORTANT

MAKE A LIST OF WHY NOT

DON'T WAIT

IT IS SOMETHING
YOU WON'T FORGET

EXPECT TO SETTLE

SEEK OUT MORE OPTIONS

FOLLOW THROUGH
ON YOUR OBLIGATIONS

DEAL WITH IT LATER

FOLLOW SOMEONE ELSE'S LEAD

MAKE A LIST OF WHY

TAKE A CHANCE

ACCEPT A CHANGE
TO YOUR ROUTINE

YOU'LL NEED TO TAKE
THE INITIATIVE

YOU'LL HAVE TO COMPROMISE

YOU'LL NEED
MORE INFORMATION

TRUST
YOUR ORIGINAL THOUGHT

IT WILL CREATE A STIR

REMOVE YOUR OWN OBSTACLES

IT WOULD BE BETTER
TO FOCUS ON YOUR WORK

IT WILL BE A PLEASURE

BE MORE GENEROUS

BET ON IT

FINISH SOMETHING ELSE FIRST

YOU MAY HAVE OPPOSITION

YOU ARE TOO CLOSE TO SEE

THE SITUATION IS UNCLEAR

A SUBSTANTIAL EFFORT
WILL BE REQUIRED

ALLOW YOURSELF TO REST FIRST

THE CHANCE WILL NOT
COME AGAIN SOON

RECONSIDER YOUR APPROACH

IT WOULD BE INADVISABLE

WAIT FOR A BETTER OFFER

SETTLE IT SOON

YES,
BUT DON'T FORCE IT

GET A CLEARER VIEW

TAKE A CHANCE

NOW YOU CAN

DON'T OVERDO IT

IT WILL SUSTAIN YOU

IT'LL COST YOU

IT IS SURE TO MAKE THINGS
INTERESTING

BE PRACTICAL

SAVE YOUR ENERGY

IT IS CERTAIN

IT IS UNCERTAIN

THE OUTCOME WILL BE POSITIVE

NO MATTER WHAT

YOU MAY HAVE TO DROP
OTHER THINGS

DON'T BE CONCERNED

PREPARE FOR THE UNEXPECTED

IT IS NOT SIGNIFICANT

TELL SOMEONE
WHAT IT MEANS TO YOU

WHATEVER YOU DO
THE RESULTS WILL BE LASTING

KEEP AN OPEN MIND

IT'S A GOOD TIME
TO MAKE PLANS

IT MAY BE DIFFICULT
BUT YOU WILL FIND VALUE IN IT

IT IS WORTH THE TROUBLE

THERE WILL BE OBSTACLES
TO OVERCOME

RELATED ISSUES MAY SURFACE

YOU ARE SURE TO HAVE SUPPORT

ASSISTANCE WOULD MAKE

YOUR PROGRESS

A SUCCESS

COLLABORATION
WILL BE THE KEY

SEEK OUT MORE OPTIONS

TAKE CHARGE

IT CANNOT FAIL

YOU MUST ACT NOW

RESPECT THE RULES

GENTLE PERSISTENCE
WILL PAY OFF

YOU WILL NOT BE DISAPPOINTED

IT MAY ALREADY BE
A DONE DEAL

FOLLOW THROUGH
WITH YOUR GOOD INTENTIONS

TAKE MORE TIME TO DECIDE

DON'T BE PRESSURED
INTO ACTING TOO QUICKLY

DON'T IGNORE THE OBVIOUS

IF YOU DON'T RESIST

IT'S NOT WORTH A STRUGGLE

DON'T FORGET TO HAVE FUN

DON'T DOUBT IT

A STRONG COMMITMENT
WILL ACHIEVE GOOD RESULTS

TRY A MORE UNLIKELY SOLUTION

LEAVE BEHIND OLD SOLUTIONS

NOT IF YOU'RE ALONE

MISHAPS ARE HIGHLY PROBABLE

PRESS FOR CLOSURE

REALIZE THAT
TOO MANY CHOICES IS AS
DIFFICULT AS TOO FEW

YES

LISTEN MORE CAREFULLY;
THEN YOU WILL KNOW

THE ANSWER
IS IN YOUR BACKYARD

LAUGH ABOUT IT

OTHERS WILL DEPEND
ON YOUR CHOICES

LET IT GO

THAT WOULD BE A WASTE
OF MONEY

GIVE IT ALL YOU'VE GOT

YOU DON'T REALLY CARE

YOU'LL NEED TO
CONSIDER OTHER WAYS

A YEAR FROM NOW
IT WON'T MATTER

DON'T WASTE YOUR TIME

IT COULD BE EXTRAORDINARY

COUNT TO 10;
ASK AGAIN

ACT AS THOUGH
IT IS ALREADY REAL

SETTING PRIORITIES
WILL BE A NECESSARY PART
OF THE PROCESS

USE YOUR IMAGINATION

IT'S GONNA BE GREAT

TO ENSURE THE BEST DECISION, BE CALM

WAIT

YOU'LL HAVE TO MAKE IT UP
AS YOU GO

YOU'LL REGRET IT

UNQUESTIONABLY

OF COURSE

YOU KNOW BETTER NOW
THAN EVER BEFORE

TRUST YOUR INTUITION

CONSIDER IT AN OPPORTUNITY

ASK YOUR FATHER

NEVER

ASK YOUR MOTHER

PERHAPS, WHEN YOU'RE OLDER

ONLY DO IT ONCE

MAYBE

NO

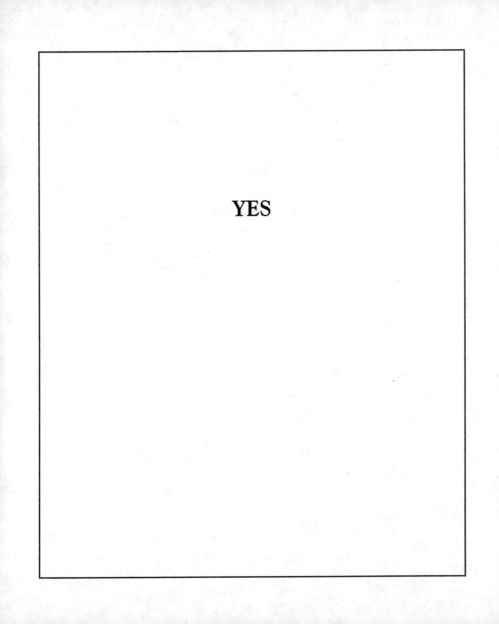

YES

YOUR ACTIONS WILL
IMPROVE THINGS

DON'T BE RIDICULOUS

DON'T BET ON IT

ADOPT
AN ADVENTUROUS ATTITUDE

FOLLOW THE ADVICE OF EXPERTS

YOU COULD FIND YOURSELF
UNABLE TO COMPROMISE

FOCUS ON YOUR HOME LIFE

INVESTIGATE
AND THEN ENJOY IT

DEFINITELY

IT WILL REMAIN UNPREDICTABLE

ABSOLUTELY NOT

EXPLORE IT
WITH PLAYFUL CURIOSITY

BE DELIGHTFULLY SURE OF IT

BETTER TO WAIT

IT SEEMS ASSURED

DO IT EARLY

THE ANSWER MAY COME TO YOU
IN ANOTHER LANGUAGE

YOU WILL NEED TO
ACCOMMODATE

DOUBT IT

IT WILL BRING GOOD LUCK

BE PATIENT

YOU WILL FIND OUT EVERYTHING
YOU'LL NEED TO KNOW

THERE IS A SUBSTANTIAL LINK
TO ANOTHER SITUATION

WATCH AND SEE WHAT HAPPENS

IT WILL AFFECT
HOW OTHERS SEE YOU

YOU'LL BE HAPPY YOU DID

GET IT IN WRITING

UNFAVORABLE AT THIS TIME

UPGRADE ANY WAY YOU CAN

IF YOU DO AS YOU'RE TOLD

IF IT'S DONE WELL;
IF NOT, DON'T DO IT AT ALL

DON'T ASK FOR ANY MORE
AT THIS TIME

AVOID THE FIRST SOLUTION

YOU'LL GET THE FINAL WORD

PROCEED AT A MORE
RELAXED PACE

THE BEST SOLUTION
MAY NOT BE THE OBVIOUS ONE

REMAIN FLEXIBLE

THAT'S OUT OF YOUR CONTROL

PROVIDED YOU SAY
"THANK YOU"

ENJOY THE EXPERIENCE

APPROACH CAUTIOUSLY

PAY ATTENTION TO THE DETAILS

WATCH YOUR STEP AS YOU GO

SPEAK UP ABOUT IT

DON'T HESITATE

THIS IS A GOOD TIME TO
MAKE A NEW PLAN

MOVE ON

THERE IS NO GUARANTEE

THE CIRCUMSTANCES
WILL CHANGE VERY QUICKLY

DON'T GET CAUGHT UP
IN YOUR EMOTIONS

SHIFT YOUR FOCUS

IT IS SIGNIFICANT

REPRIORITIZE WHAT IS IMPORTANT

MAKE A LIST OF WHY NOT

DON'T WAIT

THERE IS GOOD REASON
TO BE OPTIMISTIC

IT IS SOMETHING
YOU WON'T FORGET

NO

SEEK OUT MORE OPTIONS

FOLLOW THROUGH
ON YOUR OBLIGATIONS

DEAL WITH IT LATER

FOLLOW SOMEONE ELSE'S LEAD

MAKE A LIST OF WHY

TAKE A CHANCE

ACCEPT A CHANGE
TO YOUR ROUTINE

YOU'LL NEED TO TAKE
THE INITIATIVE

YOU'LL HAVE TO COMPROMISE

YOU'LL NEED MORE INFORMATION

TRUST
YOUR ORIGINAL THOUGHT

IT WILL CREATE A STIR

REMOVE YOUR OWN OBSTACLES

IT WOULD BE BETTER
TO FOCUS ON YOUR WORK

IT WILL BE A PLEASURE

BE MORE GENEROUS

BET ON IT

MISHAPS ARE HIGHLY PROBABLE

PRESS FOR CLOSURE

REALIZE THAT
TOO MANY CHOICES IS AS
DIFFICULT AS TOO FEW

YOU MUST

LISTEN MORE CAREFULLY;
THEN YOU WILL KNOW

THE ANSWER
IS IN YOUR BACKYARD

LAUGH ABOUT IT

OTHERS WILL DEPEND
ON YOUR CHOICES

LET IT GO

THAT WOULD BE A WASTE
OF MONEY

IT'S TIME FOR YOU TO GO

GIVE IT ALL YOU'VE GOT

YOU DON'T REALLY CARE

YOU'LL NEED TO
CONSIDER OTHER WAYS

A YEAR FROM NOW
IT WON'T MATTER

DON'T WASTE YOUR TIME

IT COULD BE EXTRAORDINARY

COUNT TO 10;
ASK AGAIN

ACT AS THOUGH
IT IS ALREADY REAL

SETTING PRIORITIES
WILL BE A NECESSARY PART
OF THE PROCESS

USE YOUR IMAGINATION

IT'S GONNA BE GREAT

TO ENSURE THE BEST DECISION,
BE CALM

WAIT

YOU'LL HAVE TO MAKE IT UP
AS YOU GO

YOU'LL REGRET IT

UNQUESTIONABLY

OF COURSE

YOU KNOW BETTER NOW
THAN EVER BEFORE

TRUST YOUR INTUITION

CONSIDER IT AN OPPORTUNITY

ASK YOUR FATHER

NEVER

ASK YOUR MOTHER

PERHAPS, WHEN YOU'RE OLDER

ONLY DO IT ONCE

MAYBE

NO

YES

FINISH SOMETHING ELSE FIRST

YOU MAY HAVE OPPOSITION

YOU ARE TOO CLOSE TO SEE

THE SITUATION IS UNCLEAR

A SUBSTANTIAL EFFORT
WILL BE REQUIRED

ALLOW YOURSELF TO REST FIRST

THE CHANCE WILL NOT
COME AGAIN SOON

RECONSIDER YOUR APPROACH

IT WOULD BE INADVISABLE

WAIT FOR A BETTER OFFER

SETTLE IT SOON

YES,
BUT DON'T FORCE IT

GET A CLEARER VIEW

TAKE A CHANCE

NOW YOU CAN

DON'T OVERDO IT

IT WILL SUSTAIN YOU

IT'LL COST YOU

IT IS SURE TO MAKE THINGS INTERESTING

BE PRACTICAL

SAVE YOUR ENERGY

IT IS CERTAIN

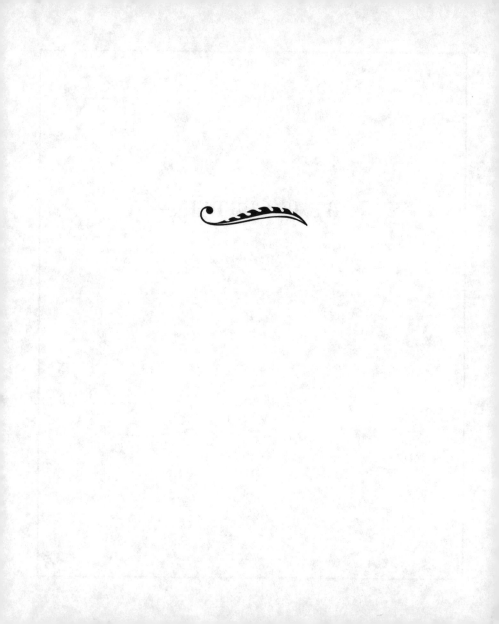

IT IS UNCERTAIN

THE OUTCOME WILL BE POSITIVE

NO MATTER WHAT

YOU MAY HAVE TO DROP
OTHER THINGS

DON'T BE CONCERNED

PREPARE FOR THE UNEXPECTED

IT IS NOT SIGNIFICANT

TELL SOMEONE
WHAT IT MEANS TO YOU

WHATEVER YOU DO
THE RESULTS WILL BE LASTING

KEEP AN OPEN MIND

IT'S A GOOD TIME
TO MAKE PLANS

IT MAY BE DIFFICULT
BUT YOU WILL FIND VALUE IN IT

IT IS WORTH THE TROUBLE

THERE WILL BE OBSTACLES
TO OVERCOME

RELATED ISSUES MAY SURFACE

YOU ARE SURE TO HAVE SUPPORT

ASSISTANCE WOULD MAKE
YOUR PROGRESS
A SUCCESS

COLLABORATION WILL BE THE KEY

SEEK OUT MORE OPTIONS

TAKE CHARGE

IT CANNOT FAIL

YOU MUST ACT NOW

RESPECT THE RULES

GENTLE PERSISTENCE
WILL PAY OFF

YOU WILL BE DISAPPOINTED

IT MAY ALREADY BE
A DONE DEAL

FOLLOW THROUGH
WITH YOUR GOOD INTENTIONS

TAKE MORE TIME TO DECIDE

DON'T BE PRESSURED
INTO ACTING TOO QUICKLY

DON'T IGNORE THE OBVIOUS

IF YOU DON'T RESIST

IT'S NOT WORTH A STRUGGLE

DON'T FORGET TO HAVE FUN

DON'T DOUBT IT

A STRONG COMMITMENT
WILL ACHIEVE GOOD RESULTS

TRY A MORE UNLIKELY SOLUTION

LEAVE BEHIND OLD SOLUTIONS

NOT IF YOU'RE ALONE

ACKNOWLEDGMENTS

From the start, the support for *The Book of Answers* has been overwhelming; and so the list of people who I thank for their support is much longer than I can fit on this page. However there are a handful who are truly special to me and to this book's evolution:

My mother and father, Doris and Bob, who have always provided me with the right answers . . . thank you.

My confidant and after-hours editor, Kris.

My friend, Sandra, for her input and ongoing support.

My island parents, Peg and Larry, who are as generous with support as they are with sincerely good times.

My literary agent, Victoria Sanders, who has the enthusiasm, leadership, and good sense of several . . . thank you for believing and following through.

My editor, Jennifer Lang, for managing all the niggly details and still finding a fresh enthusiasm.

And to my Seattle support, the list is as long as it is deep: a double tall latte of thank yous! With special gratefuls and foam to Jaq, Tim, Martha, Michael, Joshua, Barbara, Maureen, Renee, and all the staff at Boat St. Cafe.

KEEP IT TO YOURSELF

STARTLING EVENTS
MAY OCCUR AS A RESULT